getting CRAFTY

PRINTING AND STAMPING

WRITTEN BY
DANA MEACHEN RAU

45TH PARALLEL PRESS

Published in the United States of America by Cherry Lake Publishing Group
Ann Arbor, Michigan
www.cherrylakepublishing.com

Reading Adviser: Beth Walker Gambro, MS, Ed., Reading Consultant, Yorkville, IL
Illustrator: Ashley Dugan
Book Designer: Felicia Macheske

Photo Credits: © R.M. Nunes/Shutterstock, 4; © Chasham Mitra/Shutterstock, 5; © photokup/Shutterstock, 6

45th Parallel Press is an imprint of Cherry Lake Publishing Group.

Library of Congress Cataloging-in-Publication Data

Names: Rau, Dana Meachen, 1971- author. | Dugan, Ashley, illustrator.
Title: Printing and stamping / written by Dana Meachen Rau ; and illustrated by Ashley Dugan.
Description: Ann Arbor, Michigan : Cherry Lake Publishing, [2023] | Series: Getting crafty | Audience: Grades 4-6 |
    Summary: "Extra, extra, read all about getting crafty with printmaking using stamps and stencils! Discover new
    skills and learn how to make your mark with printmaking. Create patterned canvas totes, playing cards,
    wrapping paper, and more! Book includes an introduction to the different methods of printing and its history. It
    also includes several projects with easy-to-follow step-by-step instructions and illustrations. Book is developed
    to aid struggling and reluctant readers with engaging content, carefully chosen vocabulary, and simple
    sentences. Includes table of contents, glossary, index, sidebars, and author biographies"—Provided by
    publisher.
Identifiers: LCCN 2022041830 | ISBN 9781668919620 (hardcover) | ISBN 9781668920640 (paperback) |
    ISBN 9781668923306 (pdf) | ISBN 9781668921975 (ebook)
Subjects: LCSH: Prints—Technique—Juvenile literature. | Stencil work—Technique—Juvenile literature.
Classification: LCC NE860 .R38 2023 | DDC 760—dc23/eng/20220922
LC record available at https://lccn.loc.gov/2022041830

Cherry Lake Publishing Group would like to acknowledge the work of the Partnership for 21st Century Learning,
a Network of Battelle for Kids. Please visit *http://www.battelleforkids.org/networks/p21* for more information.

Printed in the United States of America
Corporate Graphics

TABLE OF CONTENTS

MAKE YOUR MARK!

Every time you touch something, you leave a mark. Your fingerprints! Your fingertips are covered with tiny ridges. The ridges have patterns. Your fingertips have oil and sweat on them. When you touch something, the oil and sweat make a print. The print is of your unique pattern. This is your fingerprint!

Artists make their own marks with prints. Printmaking is creating an image on a surface. Then **transferring** it onto another surface. A long time ago, people made handprints. They did this on cave walls. Some carved the symbols into stone. They pressed them into clay. Some carved designs into wood. They printed them onto cloth.

Printmaking kept changing. People made **plates** and **blocks**. Blocks were made from wood and metal. The blocks made images on fabric and paper. Printmaking meant you could make lots of copies. Try printing your own beautiful art!

TYPES OF PRINTS

There are three common kinds of prints. They are relief, intaglio (in-TAL-yoh), and stencil.

To make a relief print, first you carve out or build up a surface. This makes a 3D image. Then you spread ink on the image. The ink sticks to the raised areas. Place paper on top. Apply pressure. The inked areas will print onto the paper.

An intaglio print is made by carving an image. Carve it into a flat surface. Then cover the surface with ink. Make sure the ink gets into all the grooves. Wipe off the extra ink. Then put paper on top and press it down. The paper is pressed into the grooves. The paper **absorbs** the ink. Now you have a print!

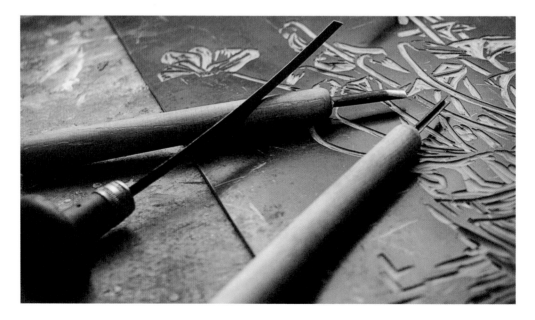

To make a stencil, cut out a shape from a sheet of plastic or paper. Put the stencil on top of printing paper. Paint on top of the stencil. Wait for it to dry. You can add more colors with more stencils.

The projects here use relief printing. They use stencils. Here are some terms to remember:

Plate or block: the surface with the image and paint

Impression: the image printed on the paper

Pulling: the act of making a print

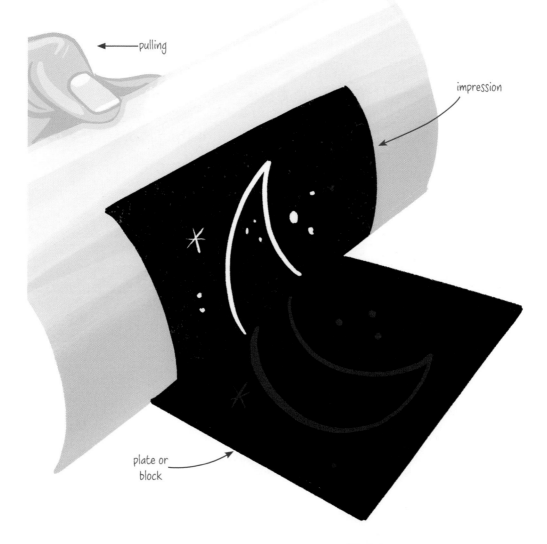

BASIC TOOLS

Printmakers use equipment. They use rollers, presses, and special inks. But you don't need all that to get started. You can use supplies that you may already have. Check at home. See what you can borrow from school.

YOU WILL NEED:

- Cutting tools: scissors, a craft knife, a paring knife, and safe cutting surfaces
- Adhesives: white glue, a hot glue gun, masking tape, and double-stick tape
- Paint and ink: washable ink pads, acrylic paint, fabric paint, paper towels, and a paper plate to use as a **palette**
- Brushes: sponge brushes, paintbrushes (Sponge brushes work best for large areas. Paintbrushes work better for smaller areas.)

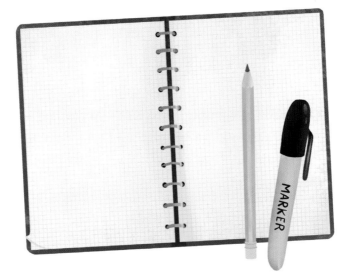

- Drawing and measuring tools: pencils, sketch paper, a ruler, a black permanent marker, and a ballpoint pen
- Material to print on: papers, plastic, fabric, newspaper, poster board, cardstock, sheets of plastic, and canvas

CARVE IT OUT OR BUILD IT UP

How do you carve a block?

You need a firm material. But it should be soft enough to be cut easily. In this book, we will use foam, potatoes, and carrots.

How do you build up a block?

You need a firm base, like craft sticks, plastic lids, or a block of wood. Then glue other materials to it. This makes a 3D image.

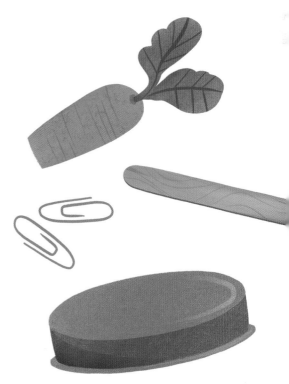

PRINTMAKING TIPS

Collect all your materials first. Make sure you have room to work. Cover your workspace with newspaper. This protects it from paint. Wear a smock or apron. This protects your clothes. Don't forget to clean up when you're done!

It may take a few tries to get your prints to come out the way you want. It takes practice. Figure out the best amount of paint. Figure out the best amount of pressure. Too much may give a muddy image. Too little may make the image too light. Print on scrap paper first.

The image you create will be backward when printed. This is important! Especially when printing letters and words. On the block or plate, letters should read from right to left. Not left to right. The letters should be flipped backward. When you pull the print, the letters will face the right way. Check your block or plate in the mirror before you use it.

Some projects here refer to a "dry brush." This means that you use just a little bit of paint. Don't use any water. Squeeze paint onto the palette. Dip just the tip of the brush in. Brush it a few times on the palette. Get rid of extra paint. Use the dry brush to apply the paint in thin layers.

Create repeating patterns! Stamp the same image a few times. Check it out!

FOUND OBJECT NOTE CARDS

Look at the world around you. It is full of cool shapes. Find small, flat objects. They can be paper clips or metal washers. They could be bits of string. Use them to make relief blocks. Print cards to send to friends and family.

MATERIALS

- Paper clips
- Metal washers
- White glue
- Large wooden craft sticks
- String
- Masking tape
- Scissors
- Cardstock paper
- Ink pads in a few colors

STEPS

1. Make a block with the paper clips or washers. Squeeze glue onto a craft stick. Place the clips or washers onto the glue. Let the glue dry.

2. Make a block with string. Tape the string to one end of a craft stick. Wind the string around the stick. Tape it along the back as you go. Trim off the extra string and tape.

3. Cut and fold the cardstock. Make a card. Press the blocks onto the ink pad. Then press them onto the card. Try using different colors. Try different patterns. Have fun!

OUTDOOR FOUND OBJECTS

Look outside! What can you find to make into a block? Ferns, leaves, and other plants can make great designs.

MUDDY PAW PRINT WRAPPING PAPER

Woof woof! **A bunch of puppies got prints all over this wrapping paper!**

MATERIALS

- Craft foam
- Scissors
- Hot glue gun
- 2 to 3 large plastic lids
- Newspaper
- Large piece of kraft paper or butcher paper
- Acrylic paint in a few colors
- Paper plate palette
- Sponge brush

STEPS

1. Use scissors. Cut out circles from the craft foam. You will make paw print stamps. Each paw print is made up of one larger circle. It has three smaller circles. You can make a few different-size paw prints.

2. Use the glue gun to attach these circles. Glue them to the flat side of the lids. You've made printing blocks!

3. Spread newspaper on your work surface. Lay the large piece of kraft paper or butcher paper on top. Put paint on your paint palette. Paint the blocks with a dry brush.

4. Press the painted blocks onto the paper. Use even pressure. Lift gently. Repeat until the paper is completely covered with paw prints. Use different sizes. Use different colors.

5. Rinse the blocks so they can be used again. Do this before the paint dries.

MONOPRINT MASTERPIECE

Most printing methods are used to create many copies of the same image. Monoprinting makes a one-of-a-kind work of art. Try different colors! Try different **textures**! What can you create?

MATERIALS

- Newspaper
- Masking tape
- Sheet of plastic
- Ink pads in a few colors
- Cotton swabs
- An old comb
- White paper

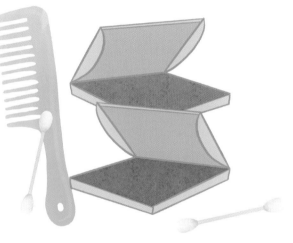

STEPS

1. Tape a piece of newspaper to your work surface. That way it won't slip around. Place the sheet of plastic on the newsprint. Tape it into place. This is the printing plate.

2. Rub and stamp the ink pads over the plate. Cover it completely. You can use one color or many. It's up to you.

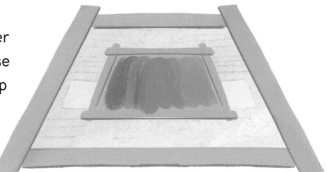

3. Add designs and textures to the plate. Do this by "drawing" on the ink. Use cotton swabs or create lines with the comb.

4. Place the paper onto the printing plate. Gently but firmly rub your hands all over the back of the paper. Slowly pull the impression from the plate.

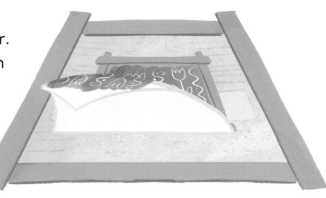

PATTERNED CANVAS CARRY-ALL

Everyone needs a useful tote bag. You can use it to carry school supplies, books, or snacks. Make your own bag to show off your style. What patterns can you come up with?!

MATERIALS

- Large potato
- Paring knife and cutting board
- Canvas bag
- Piece of cardboard (about the same size as the bag)
- Fabric paint in a few colors
- Paper plate palette
- Sponge brush
- Scrap paper

STEPS

1. Make the pattern block. Cut a potato in half. Slice pieces from the potato's sides to make a square shape.

2. Cut into the square surface. Cut at an angle. Carve out the areas you don't want to print. The raised areas will hold the paint.

Ask an adult to help you with the paring. Ask for help with craft knives. They are very sharp!

3. Place the cardboard inside the canvas bag. This will help keep the bag flat. It will keep paint from seeping through. Place the bag flat on your work surface.

4. Squeeze or pour paint onto the palette. Dip the potato block into the paint. You can also use a sponge brush to paint the block. Test out the block on scrap paper. Figure out the right amount of paint and pressure to use.

5. Paint the block again. Press it onto the bag. Repeat this over and over. Stamp straight. Stamp as close as you can to the impression next to it. If you are making the basket weave pattern, **alternate** the direction of the block each time you stamp.

6. Let the paint dry. Stamp the other side of the bag. Then let that side dry. Now you have a trendy tote!

Unlike other blocks, you can't save potato blocks for another printing! Throw those potatoes in the trash when you are done.

READ-ALL-ABOUT-IT FLYERS

People used to have to write books by hand. If they wanted to make copies, they had to write over and over. In the 1400s, movable type was invented. This is wooden or metal letters that can be placed in lines of words. These can then be printed many times. Make your own movable type! Make a flyer for an event!

MATERIALS

- Pencil
- Craft foam
- Scissors
- Craft knife and cutting surface
- Double-stick tape
- Wooden paint stirring stick
- Acrylic paint in a few colors
- Paper plate palette
- Paintbrush
- White paper

STEPS

1. Use the pencil to draw letters onto the craft foam. The letters should be about 1 inch (2.5 centimeters) tall. Cut the letters out. You can use a craft knife too. They are best for small areas.

Ask an adult to help you use a craft knife. This tool is very sharp!

2. Stick strips of double-stick tape onto the stirring stick. Place the letters along the stick. Remember you need to place them backward and from right to left. (Check them in a mirror!)

3. Paint the letters with a dry brush. Flip the stick over and hold it above the paper. Line it up where you want your words to print. Press the stick down onto the paper. Apply even pressure across the whole stick. Lift it gently. Repeat the process on as many flyers as you need. You may be able to get a few copies from the stick each time you paint it. Paint it again when your impressions start looking too faint.

4. You can use the same stirring stick for another line of type. Peel off the first set of letters and place on new ones. Rinse the letters before the paint dries. Save them to use again!

POP ART POSTER

Andy Warhol was a famous artist. He was known for his colorful artworks. He used something like stenciling. A stencil lets you ink crisp shapes over and over. You repeat the design a few times. Use different stencils. Use different inks. Warhol was known for his surprising colors. So use bright and interesting colors here!

MATERIALS

- Sketch paper
- Pencil
- Three sheets of plastic
- Black permanent marker
- Craft knife and cutting surface
- White poster board
- Ruler
- Acrylic paint (at least 4 colors)
- Paper plate palette
- Paintbrush
- Paper towels

STEPS

1. Draw a simple picture of a cupcake. Draw this on the sketch paper. Make the cupcake three parts—the bottom wrapper, the frosting, and a cherry. Place one of the plastic sheets on top of the image. Use the marker to trace it. Trace it on the other plastic sheets. Label the three stencils "wrapper," "frosting," and "cherry."

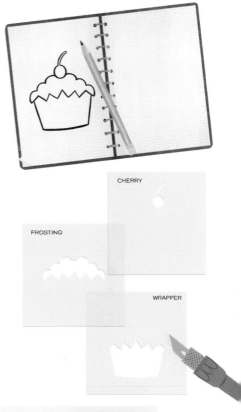

2. Cut out the wrapper area on the wrapper stencil. Use the craft knife. Then cut out the frosting part on the frosting stencil. Then cut out the cherry on the cherry stencil.

3. Measure out four squares on the poster board. The whole cupcake should fit in each square. Paint the squares. Use four different colors. Let the paint dry.

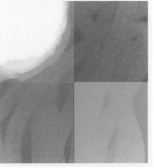

4. Place the wrapper stencil over one of the squares. Use a very dry brush. Paint within the open part of the stencil. Start near the edges. Pull the brush from the stencil onto the paper. Don't go from the paper onto the stencil. This will keep paint from getting under the stencil.

SEE NEXT PAGE

5. Use a wet paper towel. Clean off the wrapper stencil. Dry it well. Wash and dry the brush. Repeat step **4** on the next square. Use a different color. Clean the stencil and brush. Repeat on the last two squares.

WRAPPER

6. Let the paint of the wrappers dry. Repeat steps **4** and **5**. But with the frosting stencil. And then the cherry stencil.

CHERRY

RELIEF PRINT PLAYING CARDS

Woodcutting is one of the most popular ways to print. It has been used a long time. Playing cards were some of the first woodcuts to be printed on paper.

Make your own cards! Use them to play games with your friends. Woodcuts are made from wood. But this project uses foam. It is safer and easier to cut into. But the effect is the same!

MATERIALS

- Ruler
- Pencil
- Seven pieces of 8.5-inch by 11-inch (22 cm by 28 cm) cardstock paper
- Craft knife and cutting surface
- Foam tray (such as a fruit or veggie tray from a grocery store)
- Scissors
- Scrap paper
- Masking tape
- Ballpoint pen
- Acrylic paint (red, black, and a third color of your choice)
- Paper plate palette
- Sponge brush
- 4 large carrots
- Paring knife and cutting board
- Toothpicks

SEE NEXT PAGE

STEPS

1. Use the ruler and pencil. Measure and mark eight equal rectangles. Do this on all the pieces of cardstock paper. Each rectangle will be 4.25 inches by 2.75 inches (10.8 cm by 7 cm). Set the paper aside.

2. Use the craft knife to cut a rectangle out of the foam tray. It should measure about 4.25 inches by 2.75 inches (10.8 cm by 7 cm). Use scissors to cut out a piece of scrap paper. Make it about the same size as the foam piece. Draw a simple picture on the paper. Draw it in the opposite way you want it to appear. Tape it face up on the foam.

3. Use the pen to trace over all the lines of the image. Press down gently. You're transferring the lines of the picture onto the foam. Remove the paper. Trace over the indented lines on the foam again. Use more pressure. Cut more deeply into the foam. This is your printing block.

4. Paint the block with a dry brush. Press the painted block onto the cardstock. Do it within the lines of one of the rectangles. Apply even pressure. Lift the block gently. Repeat until you have filled in the rest of the rectangles. Then repeat on the other 6 pieces of marked cardstock. You will have 56 impressions in all. That's enough for a deck of 52 cards. Plus some extra if you make a mistake. Let them dry. Cut along all the lines to make cards.

5. For the other side of the cards, you will carve blocks out of carrots. You will be making seven blocks. Four will be the **suits**. Those are hearts, diamonds, clubs, and spades. You'll also need a K, Q, and J. That is for Kings, Queens, and Jacks. Cut the carrots in half. Draw on the flat surfaces of the cut carrots. Use toothpicks to draw. Draw the shapes and letters you need. Use a knife to cut away pieces of the carrot around the drawing. Carve the letters backward!

SEE NEXT PAGE

6. The hearts and diamonds on your cards should be red. The spades and clubs should be black. The K, Q, and J will need to be both red and black. Start with the suits. Dip a block into the paint. **Blot** it on scrap paper. Get rid of excess paint. Stamp it onto the cards. Stamp once for the ace. Stamp twice for the 2 card. Stamp three times for the 3 card. Continue like this until you reach 10. For the Kings, Queens, and Jacks, stamp each card once with a suit and once with the K, Q, or J. Use the right color for each suit. Rinse the blocks before switching colors.

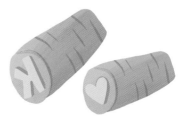

Rinse the foam block when the paint is still wet. You can use it for another project. But throw away the carrot blocks when you are done!

ONE OF A KIND

Printing takes practice. Don't worry if your prints aren't perfect. Even after lots of tries! Art is about trying new things. It's about unplanned creations. Be daring! Be an artist!

Pull multiple images from a plate or block. The impressions will all be a little different—even if you print 100 copies! Some may be muddled. Some may be faint. Some may be perfect. However they come out, they will all be unique. Every impression is one of a kind. Just like you!

GLOSSARY

absorb (uhb-ZORB) to soak up

alternate (AHL-tuhr-nayt) go back and forth between two directions

blocks (BLAHKS) surfaces that hold ink or paint in the printing process

blot (BLAHT) to dry by soaking up excess liquid

impression (im-PREH-shuhn) an image created through a printing process

muddled (MUH-duhld) mixed up or unclear

palette (PAH-luht) a flat surface for holding or mixing paint

plates (PLAYTS) surfaces that hold ink or paint in the printing process

suits (SOOTS) the symbols used on playing cards

textures (TEKS-churz) the different ways things feel, such as how rough or smooth they are

transferring (trans-FUHR-ing) moving from one place to another

FOR MORE INFORMATION

BOOKS

Hanson, Anders. *Cool Printmaking*. Edina, MN: ABDO Publishing Company, 2009.

Medina, Sarah. *Having Fun With Printing*. New York: PowerKids Press, 2008.

Powell, Michelle. *Printing*. Chicago: Heinemann Library, 2000.

Rhatigan, Joe, and Rain Newcomb. *Stamp It!* New York: Lark Books, 2004.

Schwake, Susan. *Art Lab for Kids: 52 Creative Adventures in Drawing, Painting, Printmaking, Paper, and Mixed Media—for Budding Artists of All Ages*. Beverly, MA: Quarry Books, 2012.

INDEX